FIND YOUR BLISS

2023
WEEKLY PLANNER
JULY 2022 • DECEMBER 2023

ROCK
POINT

2023 Year at a Glance

JANUARY

S	M	T	W	T	F	S
1	2	3	4	5	6	7
8	9	10	11	12	13	14
15	16	17	18	19	20	21
22	23	24	25	26	27	28
29	30	31				

FEBRUARY

S	M	T	W	T	F	S
			1	2	3	4
5	6	7	8	9	10	11
12	13	14	15	16	17	18
19	20	21	22	23	24	25
26	27	28				

MARCH

S	M	T	W	T	F	S
			1	2	3	4
5	6	7	8	9	10	11
12	13	14	15	16	17	18
19	20	21	22	23	24	25
26	27	28	29	30	31	

APRIL

S	M	T	W	T	F	S
						1
2	3	4	5	6	7	8
9	10	11	12	13	14	15
16	17	18	19	20	21	22
23	24	25	26	27	28	29
30						

MAY

S	M	T	W	T	F	S
	1	2	3	4	5	6
7	8	9	10	11	12	13
14	15	16	17	18	19	20
21	22	23	24	25	26	27
28	29	30	31			

JUNE

S	M	T	W	T	F	S
				1	2	3
4	5	6	7	8	9	10
11	12	13	14	15	16	17
18	19	20	21	22	23	24
25	26	27	28	29	30	

JULY

S	M	T	W	T	F	S
						1
2	3	4	5	6	7	8
9	10	11	12	13	14	15
16	17	18	19	20	21	22
23	24	25	26	27	28	29
30	31					

AUGUST

S	M	T	W	T	F	S
		1	2	3	4	5
6	7	8	9	10	11	12
13	14	15	16	17	18	19
20	21	22	23	24	25	26
27	28	29	30	31		

SEPTEMBER

S	M	T	W	T	F	S
					1	2
3	4	5	6	7	8	9
10	11	12	13	14	15	16
17	18	19	20	21	22	23
24	25	26	27	28	29	30

OCTOBER

S	M	T	W	T	F	S
1	2	3	4	5	6	7
8	9	10	11	12	13	14
15	16	17	18	19	20	21
22	23	24	25	26	27	28
29	30	31				

NOVEMBER

S	M	T	W	T	F	S
			1	2	3	4
5	6	7	8	9	10	11
12	13	14	15	16	17	18
19	20	21	22	23	24	25
26	27	28	29	30		

DECEMBER

S	M	T	W	T	F	S
					1	2
3	4	5	6	7	8	9
10	11	12	13	14	15	16
17	18	19	20	21	22	23
24	25	26	27	28	29	30
31						

2024 Year at a Glance

JANUARY

S	M	T	W	T	F	S
	1	2	3	4	5	6
7	8	9	10	11	12	13
14	15	16	17	18	19	20
21	22	23	24	25	26	27
28	29	30	31			

FEBRUARY

S	M	T	W	T	F	S
				1	2	3
4	5	6	7	8	9	10
11	12	13	14	15	16	17
18	19	20	21	22	23	24
25	26	27	28	29		

MARCH

S	M	T	W	T	F	S
					1	2
3	4	5	6	7	8	9
10	11	12	13	14	15	16
17	18	19	20	21	22	23
24	25	26	27	28	29	30
31						

APRIL

S	M	T	W	T	F	S
	1	2	3	4	5	6
7	8	9	10	11	12	13
14	15	16	17	18	19	20
21	22	23	24	25	26	27
28	29	30				

MAY

S	M	T	W	T	F	S
			1	2	3	4
5	6	7	8	9	10	11
12	13	14	15	16	17	18
19	20	21	22	23	24	25
26	27	28	29	30	31	

JUNE

S	M	T	W	T	F	S
						1
2	3	4	5	6	7	8
9	10	11	12	13	14	15
16	17	18	19	20	21	22
23	24	25	26	27	28	29
30						

JULY

S	M	T	W	T	F	S
	1	2	3	4	5	6
7	8	9	10	11	12	13
14	15	16	17	18	19	20
21	22	23	24	25	26	27
28	29	30	31			

AUGUST

S	M	T	W	T	F	S
				1	2	3
4	5	6	7	8	9	10
11	12	13	14	15	16	17
18	19	20	21	22	23	24
25	26	27	28	29	30	31

SEPTEMBER

S	M	T	W	T	F	S
1	2	3	4	5	6	7
8	9	10	11	12	13	14
15	16	17	18	19	20	21
22	23	24	25	26	27	28
29	30					

OCTOBER

S	M	T	W	T	F	S
		1	2	3	4	5
6	7	8	9	10	11	12
13	14	15	16	17	18	19
20	21	22	23	24	25	26
27	28	29	30	31		

NOVEMBER

S	M	T	W	T	F	S
					1	2
3	4	5	6	7	8	9
10	11	12	13	14	15	16
17	18	19	20	21	22	23
24	25	26	27	28	29	30

DECEMBER

S	M	T	W	T	F	S
1	2	3	4	5	6	7
8	9	10	11	12	13	14
15	16	17	18	19	20	21
22	23	24	25	26	27	28
29	30	31				

LIVE INSPIRED

Everything
begins from
a moment
of inspiration.

JULY 2022

NOTES	SUNDAY	MONDAY	TUESDAY
	3	4	5
		INDEPENDENCE DAY (US)	
	10	11	12
	17	18	19
	24	25	26
	31		

JULY 2022

WEDNESDAY	THURSDAY	FRIDAY	SATURDAY
		1	2
		CANADA DAY (CAN)	
6	7	8	9
13	14	15	16
20	21	22	23
27	28	29	30

"Life is about taking risks.
If you play your life safe
and you don't take risks,
you're going to live
your life at a low hum.
That might be fine
for certain people,
but I don't want to live
my life at a low hum.
I want to live my life
proud and loud and
to the fullest expression
that I possibly can."

ROBBIE BRENNER

Oscar®-nominated Producer,
Executive VP and Producer, Mattel Films

JULY 2022

MONDAY (JUNE)	**27**
TUESDAY (JUNE)	**28**
WEDNESDAY (JUNE)	**29**
THURSDAY (JUNE)	**30**
FRIDAY CANADA DAY (CAN)	**1**
SATURDAY	**2**
SUNDAY	**3**

JULY 2022

MONDAY INDEPENDENCE DAY (US)   4

TUESDAY   5

WEDNESDAY   6

THURSDAY   7

FRIDAY 8

SATURDAY 9

SUNDAY 10

> Living inspired means paying attention to the things that excite you, the things that give you butterflies, the things that make you a little more curious about the world.

JULY 2022

MONDAY   **11**

TUESDAY   **12**

WEDNESDAY ●   **13**

THURSDAY   **14**

FRIDAY   15

SATURDAY   16

SUNDAY   17

When you're teetering on the edge of success
and failure, amazing things can happen.
Find things that excite you and go for them.
Follow your instincts.

JULY 2022

MONDAY 18

TUESDAY 19

WEDNESDAY ◐ 20

THURSDAY 21

FRIDAY   22

SATURDAY   23

SUNDAY   24

Inspiration is everywhere and anywhere
we choose to seek it, and it often happens
in the moments we are still and present.

JULY 2022

MONDAY 25

TUESDAY 26

WEDNESDAY 27

THURSDAY ○ 28

FRIDAY 29

SATURDAY 30

SUNDAY 31

Not knowing where to begin is actually
the best place to begin;
you can start with a clean slate.
When things are unknown, anything is possible.

BE
BOLD

Your boldness will become a beacon for others.

AUGUST 2022

NOTES	SUNDAY	MONDAY	TUESDAY
		1	2
		SUMMER BANK HOLIDAY (UK-SCT)	
	7	8	9
	14	15	16
	21	22	23
	28	29	30
		SUMMER BANK HOLIDAY (UK-ENG / NIR / WAL)	

AUGUST 2022

WEDNESDAY	THURSDAY	FRIDAY	SATURDAY
3	4 ☽	5	6
10 ●	11	12	13
17	18 ☽	19	20
24	25	26 ○	27
31			

"**You need to listen** to your gut and go at your own pace. There's a ton of wisdom in previous ways of doing things, but it's also always changing and evolving. How you approach things needs to be entirely your own."

DIANNA COHEN

Founder and CEO of Crown Affair

AUGUST 2022

MONDAY SUMMER BANK HOLIDAY (UK-SCT) 1

TUESDAY 2

WEDNESDAY 3

THURSDAY 4

FRIDAY ☽ 5

SATURDAY 6

SUNDAY 7

AUGUST 2022

MONDAY 8

TUESDAY 9

WEDNESDAY 10

THURSDAY 11

FRIDAY 12

SATURDAY 13

SUNDAY 14

Live in your truth,
and have the confidence and courage
to take a stand for something
you believe in.

AUGUST 2022

MONDAY 15

TUESDAY 16

WEDNESDAY 17

THURSDAY 18

FRIDAY ☽   **19**

SATURDAY   **20**

SUNDAY   **21**

Boldness isn't a given: it's a choice.
We can choose to stay small and comfortable
or we can step out of our comfort zone
and experience everything the world has to offer.

AUGUST 2022

MONDAY   22

TUESDAY   23

WEDNESDAY   24

THURSDAY   25

FRIDAY   26

SATURDAY ○   27

SUNDAY   28

Go after your dreams.
Be bold knowing that
there is a sisterhood of freethinking,
strong women right beside you.

HEART OF GOLD

Cultivate a kind heart, and your legacy will be golden.

SEPTEMBER 2022

NOTES	SUNDAY	MONDAY	TUESDAY
	4	**5**	**6**
	FATHER'S DAY (AUS / NZ)	LABOR DAY (US) LABOUR DAY (CAN)	
	11	**12**	**13**
	PATRIOT DAY (US) GRANDPARENTS' DAY (US)		
	18	**19**	**20**
	○ **25**	**26**	**27**
	ROSH HASHANAH (BEGINS AT SUNDOWN)		

SEPTEMBER 2022

WEDNESDAY	THURSDAY	FRIDAY	SATURDAY
	1	2 ◖	3
7	8	9 ●	10
14	15	16 ◗	17
	FIRST DAY OF NATIONAL HISPANIC HERITAGE MONTH		
21	22	23	24
	FALL EQUINOX		
28	29	30	

"Abandon all the expectations everyone has of you and any **ambition of being perfect.** Use your incredibly powerful voice. Even if it makes others uncomfortable. Especially if it makes others uncomfortable."

MANDANA DAYANI

Creator and Cofounder of I Am a Voter,
Cohost of The Dissenters Podcast,
Attorney, and Angel Investor

SEPTEMBER 2022

MONDAY (AUGUST) SUMMER BANK HOLIDAY (UK-ENG / NIR / WAL) — **29**

TUESDAY (AUGUST) — **30**

WEDNESDAY (AUGUST) — **31**

THURSDAY — **1**

FRIDAY — **2**

SATURDAY ◖ — **3**

SUNDAY FATHER'S DAY (AUS / NZ) — **4**

SEPTEMBER 2022

MONDAY LABOR DAY (US) / LABOUR DAY (CAN)   **5**

TUESDAY   **6**

WEDNESDAY   **7**

THURSDAY   **8**

FRIDAY   9

SATURDAY ●   10

SUNDAY   PATRIOT DAY (US) / GRANDPARENTS' DAY (US)   11

**The most beautiful legacy
you can leave behind
is your kindness and generosity.**

SEPTEMBER 2022

MONDAY 12

TUESDAY 13

WEDNESDAY 14

THURSDAY NATIONAL HISPANIC HERITAGE MONTH BEGINS 15

FRIDAY   16

SATURDAY ☽   17

SUNDAY   18

If you act from a place of love, that love will come back to you. Never underestimate the power of a handwritten note or going the extra mile for others. Love begets love. Heart begets heart. Be a catalyst for positivity in the world.

SEPTEMBER 2022

MONDAY 19

TUESDAY 20

WEDNESDAY 21

THURSDAY FALL EQUINOX 22

FRIDAY 23

SATURDAY 24

SUNDAY   ROSH HASHANAH (BEGINS AT SUNDOWN)   ○   25

Focus on the quality of your intentions,
not the quantity of your achievements.
How you treat others lays the foundation of your life.

POWER
FUL

You are
more powerful
than you realize.
Tremendous
inner strength
and uniqueness
lie inside of you;
all you
have to do is
harness it.

OCTOBER 2022

NOTES	SUNDAY	MONDAY	TUESDAY
	◐ 2	3	4
		LABOUR DAY (AUS-ACT / NSW / SA)	YOM KIPPUR (BEGINS AT SUNDOWN)
	● 9	10	11
	SUKKOT (BEGINS AT SUNDOWN)	INDIGENOUS PEOPLES' DAY (US) COLUMBUS DAY (US) THANKSGIVING DAY (CAN)	
	16	◑ 17	18
		SIMCHAT TORAH (BEGINS AT SUNDOWN)	
	23	24	○ 25
		LABOUR DAY (NZ)	
	30	31	
		HALLOWEEN	

OCTOBER 2022

WEDNESDAY	THURSDAY	FRIDAY	SATURDAY
			1
5	6	7	8
12	13	14	15
19	20	21	22
26	27	28	29

"**I can't control my body,**
but I absolutely have the power
to control my thoughts.
Life doesn't always
give you what you want.
But it gives you what you need,
to mold you, to hurt you,
and to gradually strengthen you
into the person you were
meant to become."

GAYLYN HENDERSON

Founder of Gutless and Glamorous

OCTOBER 2022

MONDAY (SEPTEMBER)   **26**

TUESDAY (SEPTEMBER)   **27**

WEDNESDAY (SEPTEMBER)   **28**

THURSDAY (SEPTEMBER)   **29**

FRIDAY (SEPTEMBER)   **30**

SATURDAY   **1**

SUNDAY   **2**

OCTOBER 2022

MONDAY LABOUR DAY (AUS-ACT / NSW / SA) 3

TUESDAY YOM KIPPUR (BEGINS AT SUNDOWN) 4

WEDNESDAY 5

THURSDAY 6

FRIDAY   7

SATURDAY   8

SUNDAY SUKKOT (BEGINS AT SUNDOWN)   9

> Being your unapologetically authentic self and
> embracing your individuality is the most powerful thing
> you can do in a world that tells us what to look like,
> what to wear, what to be, and what to believe.

OCTOBER 2022

MONDAY INDIGENOUS PEOPLES' DAY (US) / COLUMBUS DAY (US) / THANKSGIVING DAY (CAN)   **10**

TUESDAY   **11**

WEDNESDAY   **12**

THURSDAY   **13**

FRIDAY   **14**

SATURDAY   **15**

SUNDAY   **16**

No one has ever experienced the world exactly as you have. When we begin to think deeply about who we are beneath the layers and labels, our power emerges.

OCTOBER 2022

MONDAY SIMCHAT TORAH (BEGINS AT SUNDOWN) **17**

TUESDAY **18**

WEDNESDAY **19**

THURSDAY **20**

FRIDAY   21

SATURDAY   22

SUNDAY   23

Never underestimate the value you bring to the world.
Allow yourself to be vulnerable, raw, and real,
and you'll be amazed at the powerful connections
you make with others.

OCTOBER 2022

MONDAY LABOUR DAY (NZ) 24

TUESDAY ○ 25

WEDNESDAY 26

THURSDAY 27

FRIDAY   28

SATURDAY   29

SUNDAY   30

The strongest actions for a woman is to love herself,
be herself and shine amongst those
who never believed she could.

THINK POSITIVE

We become
what we think about. Believe in the power of your own thoughts and manifest your destiny.

NOVEMBER 2022

NOTES	SUNDAY	MONDAY	TUESDAY
			1
			ALL SAINTS' DAY
	6	7	8
	DAYLIGHT SAVING TIME ENDS (US / CAN)		ELECTION DAY (US)
	13	14	15
	20	21	22
	27	28	29

NOVEMBER 2022

WEDNESDAY	THURSDAY	FRIDAY	SATURDAY
2	3	4	5
9	10	11 VETERANS DAY (US)	12
☽ 16	17	18	19
○ 23	24 THANKSGIVING DAY (US)	25 NATIVE AMERICAN HERITAGE DAY (US)	26
30			

"You can't make a wrong choice, everything will inform. **There are no wrongs.** On the other side of fear is oftentimes connection and self-esteem. You're worth it. We're capable of doing things that are really uncomfortable."

TAYLOR SCHILLING

Award-winning Actor, Golden Globe Nominee

NOVEMBER 2022

MONDAY (OCTOBER) HALLOWEEN — 31

TUESDAY ALL SAINTS' DAY — 1

WEDNESDAY — 2

THURSDAY — 3

FRIDAY — 4

SATURDAY — 5

SUNDAY DAYLIGHT SAVING TIME ENDS (US / CAN) — 6

NOVEMBER 2022

MONDAY 7

TUESDAY ELECTION DAY (US) ● 8

WEDNESDAY 9

THURSDAY 10

FRIDAY VETERANS DAY (US)   **11**

SATURDAY   **12**

SUNDAY   **13**

We can't allow ourselves to get so caught up
in "arriving" that we fail to appreciate the journey
of "getting there." With a positive mind-set,
a grateful heart, and a clear focus,
you can become a force to be reckoned with.

NOVEMBER 2022

MONDAY   **14**

TUESDAY   **15**

WEDNESDAY ◗   **16**

THURSDAY   **17**

FRIDAY **18**

SATURDAY **19**

SUNDAY **20**

**To think positively
is to focus our energy on the things
that ignite excitement, gratitude,
and love within us.**

NOVEMBER 2022

MONDAY 21

TUESDAY 22

WEDNESDAY ○ 23

THURSDAY THANKSGIVING DAY (US) 24

FRIDAY NATIVE AMERICAN HERITAGE DAY (US) **25**

SATURDAY **26**

SUNDAY **27**

Optimism will get you so much farther in life than pessimism ever will. It's the ability to reframe any circumstance we're in to find the silver lining rather than focus on the dark cloud.

PERSEVERANCE

To persevere
is to commit with unwavering patience and desire to see your dreams through.

DECEMBER 2022

NOTES	SUNDAY	MONDAY	TUESDAY
	4	5	6
	11	12	13
	18	19	20
	HANUKKAH (BEGINS AT SUNDOWN) 25	26	27
	CHRISTMAS DAY	BOXING DAY (UK /CAN / AUS / NZ) KWANZAA	

DECEMBER 2022

WEDNESDAY	THURSDAY	FRIDAY	SATURDAY
	1	2	3
	WORLD AIDS DAY		INTERNATIONAL DAY OF PERSONS WITH DISABILITIES
7	8	9	10
			HUMAN RIGHTS DAY
14	15	16	17
21	22	23	24
WINTER SOLSTICE			CHRISTMAS EVE
28	29	30	31
			NEW YEAR'S EVE

"Don't quit.
It implies you've
already started—which
most of us have in some way,
even if our ideas
are still just daydreams.
But the truth is simple;
if you don't quit,
you will succeed."

ELIZA BLANK

Founder and CEO of The Sill

DECEMBER 2022

MONDAY (NOVEMBER)   **28**

TUESDAY (NOVEMBER)   **29**

WEDNESDAY (NOVEMBER)   **30**

THURSDAY   WORLD AIDS DAY   **1**

FRIDAY   **2**

SATURDAY   INTERNATIONAL DAY OF PERSONS WITH DISABILITIES   **3**

SUNDAY   **4**

DECEMBER 2022

MONDAY 5

TUESDAY 6

WEDNESDAY 7

THURSDAY 8

FRIDAY 9

SATURDAY HUMAN RIGHTS DAY 10

SUNDAY 11

Perseverance is learning to transform
the low moments into forward motion.
It's fighting the urge to quit.
It's believing in something bigger.

DECEMBER 2022

MONDAY 12

TUESDAY 13

WEDNESDAY 14

THURSDAY 15

FRIDAY ☽ 16

SATURDAY 17

SUNDAY HANUKKAH (BEGINS AT SUNDOWN) 18

The most beautiful things can come from
the hardest of circumstances. You must grow
through what you go through in your life
to become the beautiful person you're meant to be.

DECEMBER 2022

MONDAY

19

TUESDAY

20

WEDNESDAY   WINTER SOLSTICE

21

THURSDAY

22

FRIDAY ○   **23**

SATURDAY CHRISTMAS EVE   **24**

SUNDAY CHRISTMAS DAY   **25**

> If you do something long enough, if you truly commit,
> you will find success on any path you pursue.
> Let your passion pull you through the mud,
> and you'll always find your way.

EMB
RACE
CHANGE

Trust the magic of change and new beginnings.

JANUARY 2023

NOTES	SUNDAY	MONDAY	TUESDAY
	1	2	3
	NEW YEAR'S DAY	BANK HOLIDAY (UK-SCT)	
	8	9	10
	15	16	17
		CIVIL RIGHTS DAY MARTIN LUTHER KING JR. DAY (US)	
	22	23	24
	CHINESE NEW YEAR		
	29	30	31

JANUARY 2023

WEDNESDAY	THURSDAY	FRIDAY	SATURDAY
4	5 ●	6	7
11	12	13 ◗	14
18	19	20 ○	21
25	26 AUSTRALIA DAY	27 ◖ HOLOCAUST REMEMBRANCE DAY	28

"The feeling of change is all-encompassing. Try to embrace it instead of fear it! It's exciting to feel that these decisions and moments in your life can really shape your future, and when you look back on them you will remember the confidence you felt facing them."

KELSIE HAYES

Founder and CEO of POPUP FLORIST

JANUARY 2023

MONDAY (DECEMBER) BOXING DAY
(UK / CAN / AUS / NZ) / KWANZAA **26**

TUESDAY (DECEMBER) **27**

WEDNESDAY (DECEMBER) **28**

THURSDAY (DECEMBER) ◖ **29**

FRIDAY (DECEMBER) **30**

SATURDAY (DECEMBER) NEW YEAR'S EVE **31**

SUNDAY NEW YEAR'S DAY **1**

JANUARY 2023

MONDAY BANK HOLIDAY (UK-SCT)   2

TUESDAY   3

WEDNESDAY   4

THURSDAY   5

FRIDAY ● **6**

SATURDAY **7**

SUNDAY **8**

Each chapter of our lives
will bring new challenges and growth opportunities.
It's up to us whether we let our doubts stagnate us
or embrace the change with open arms.

JANUARY 2023

MONDAY   9

TUESDAY   10

WEDNESDAY   11

THURSDAY   12

FRIDAY

13

SATURDAY ☽

14

SUNDAY

15

Extraordinary things can happen in the space between who you are and who you are becoming. Embrace change, because in this crazy, ever-evolving life, we could all do with a little more magic.

JANUARY 2023

MONDAY CIVIL RIGHTS DAY / MARTIN LUTHER KING JR. DAY (US) **16**

TUESDAY **17**

WEDNESDAY **18**

THURSDAY **19**

FRIDAY   20

SATURDAY ○   21

SUNDAY CHINESE NEW YEAR   22

You are never *stuck* and your past
does not have to define who you become.
We have more power than we realize
to change ourselves and our circumstances.

JANUARY 2023

MONDAY   23

TUESDAY   24

WEDNESDAY   25

THURSDAY   AUSTRALIA DAY   26

FRIDAY HOLOCAUST REMEMBRANCE DAY   **27**

SATURDAY ◖   **28**

SUNDAY   **29**

The successful have proven that in order to reach
greatness you need to keep on improving yourself.
Skill up, investing in yourself is the greatest
investment you can ever make.

Saying yes opens your heart, mind, and spirit to a world of possibilities beyond what you imagined.

FEBRUARY 2023

NOTES	SUNDAY	MONDAY	TUESDAY
	5	**6**	**7**
	WAITANGI DAY (NZ)	WAITANGI DAY OBSERVED (NZ)	
	12	**13**	**14**
			VALENTINE'S DAY
	19	**20**	**21**
		PRESIDENTS' DAY (US)	
	26	**27**	**28**

FEBRUARY 2023

WEDNESDAY	THURSDAY	FRIDAY	SATURDAY
1 FIRST DAY OF BLACK HISTORY MONTH	2 GROUNDHOG DAY (US / CAN)	3	4
8	9	10	11
15	16	17	18
22 ASH WEDNESDAY	23	24	25

"People reinvent themselves
in every decade and you never know
where your life can take you.
The number one thing
you can work on within your control
is how you see the world
and its opportunities.
Your positive energy will carry you
through and make you a star
in whatever you decide to do."

MEGHAN ASHA

Founder and CEO of FounderMade

FEBRUARY 2023

MONDAY (JANUARY)   **30**

TUESDAY (JANUARY)   **31**

WEDNESDAY FIRST DAY OF BLACK HISTORY MONTH   **1**

THURSDAY GROUNDHOG DAY (US / CAN)   **2**

FRIDAY   **3**

SATURDAY   **4**

SUNDAY WAITANGI DAY (NZ)   **5**

FEBRUARY 2023

MONDAY WAITANGI DAY OBSERVED (NZ) **6**

TUESDAY **7**

WEDNESDAY **8**

THURSDAY **9**

FRIDAY   10

SATURDAY   11

SUNDAY   12

Sometimes you have to jump in,
say "yes," and figure things out afterward.
Pushing yourself to these "sink or swim" moments
is sometimes the necessary fire you need
to kick things into high gear.

FEBRUARY 2023

MONDAY ☽   **13**

TUESDAY VALENTINE'S DAY   **14**

WEDNESDAY   **15**

THURSDAY   **16**

FRIDAY   17

SATURDAY   18

SUNDAY   19

When you live your life with a "yes" mentality,
you open your mind, heart, and spirit to a world
of possibilities beyond what you imagined. Every
person is a door to a new world, and every person
you'll ever meet knows something that you don't.

FEBRUARY 2023

MONDAY PRESIDENTS' DAY (US) ○ **20**

TUESDAY **21**

WEDNESDAY ASH WEDNESDAY **22**

THURSDAY **23**

FRIDAY   24

SATURDAY   25

SUNDAY   26

The most interesting people have gotten where they are
because they said "yes" at some point in time
to something out of their comfort zone.
What can you say "yes" to that you've been
avoiding or not feeling ready for?

MOVE
MOUN
TAINS

Set your heart on it and there will be no mountain you can't move.

MARCH 2023

NOTES	SUNDAY	MONDAY	TUESDAY
	5	**6** ●	**7**
		PURIM (BEGINS AT SUNDOWN)	
	12	**13**	**14**
	DAYLIGHT SAVING TIME BEGINS (US / CAN)	LABOUR DAY (AUS-VIC)	
	19	**20** ○	**21**
	MOTHERING SUNDAY (UK)	SPRING EQUINOX	NOWRUZ
	26	**27** ☽	**28**

MARCH 2023

WEDNESDAY	THURSDAY	FRIDAY	SATURDAY
1 FIRST DAY OF WOMEN'S HISTORY MONTH	2	3	4
8	9	10	11
15	16	17 ST. PATRICK'S DAY	18
22 RAMADAN (BEGINS AT SUNDOWN)	23	24	25
29	30	31	

"It's not about
moving one mountain;
it's about moving a mountain range.
You're going to get over one
and have to set sights on another.
Surround yourself with people
you want to join in your journey.
Build a community
that you want to hike with."

BECKY STRAW

Cofounder and CEO of The Adventure Project

MARCH 2023

MONDAY (FEBRUARY) 27

TUESDAY (FEBRUARY) 28

WEDNESDAY FIRST DAY OF WOMEN'S HISTORY MONTH 1

THURSDAY 2

FRIDAY 3

SATURDAY 4

SUNDAY 5

MARCH 2023

MONDAY PURIM (BEGINS AT SUNDOWN)   **6**

TUESDAY ●   **7**

WEDNESDAY   **8**

THURSDAY   **9**

FRIDAY 10

SATURDAY 11

SUNDAY DAYLIGHT SAVING TIME BEGINS (US / CAN) 12

Life gives us a series of mountains we have to climb.
They're put on our path
to test us, teach us, and strengthen our will.

MARCH 2023

MONDAY LABOUR DAY (AUS-VIC)   13

TUESDAY   14

WEDNESDAY ☽   15

THURSDAY   16

FRIDAY ST. PATRICK'S DAY $\qquad$ **17**

SATURDAY $\qquad$ **18**

SUNDAY MOTHERING SUNDAY (UK) $\qquad$ **19**

With each mountain we climb and conquer,
we increase our threshold and ability to handle
even harder climbs and more treacherous paths.
We develop confidence in our ability to overcome.

MARCH 2023

MONDAY SPRING EQUINOX   **20**

TUESDAY NOWRUZ ○   **21**

WEDNESDAY RAMADAN (BEGINS AT SUNDOWN)   **22**

THURSDAY   **23**

FRIDAY 24

SATURDAY 25

SUNDAY 26

Most things in life worth having are hard won.
The mountains we face strengthen our ability
to dream and work toward something greater.

Our failures are our greatest teachers.

APRIL 2023

NOTES	SUNDAY	MONDAY	TUESDAY
	2	3	4
	PALM SUNDAY		
	9	10	11
	EASTER		
	16	17	18
	ORTHODOX EASTER	YOM HASHOAH (BEGINS AT SUNDOWN)	
	23	24	25
	30		ANZAC DAY (AUS / NZ)

APRIL 2023

WEDNESDAY	THURSDAY	FRIDAY	SATURDAY
			1 APRIL FOOLS' DAY
5 PASSOVER (BEGINS AT SUNDOWN)	**6** ●	**7** GOOD FRIDAY	**8**
12 ◗	**13**	**14**	**15**
19 ○	**20**	**21** EID AL-FITR (BEGINS AT SUNDOWN)	**22** EARTH DAY
26 ◖ ADMINISTRATIVE PROFESSIONALS' DAY (US)	**27**	**28**	**29**

"It took several years
and starting my own company
to realize that the only person
standing in my way
of achieving my dreams was me.
You don't need specific diplomas
or fancy endorsements
to prove your worth.
**The grit, the passion,
the resilience ultimately
come from within.**"

CAMERON ARMSTRONG

Founder and CEO of Kitty and Vibe

APRIL 2023

MONDAY (MARCH)   **27**

TUESDAY (MARCH) ☽   **28**

WEDNESDAY (MARCH)   **29**

THURSDAY (MARCH)   **30**

FRIDAY (MARCH)   **31**

SATURDAY APRIL FOOLS' DAY   **1**

SUNDAY PALM SUNDAY   **2**

APRIL 2023

MONDAY 3

TUESDAY 4

WEDNESDAY PASSOVER (BEGINS AT SUNDOWN) 5

THURSDAY ● 6

FRIDAY GOOD FRIDAY 7

SATURDAY 8

SUNDAY EASTER 9

Our rejections and failures can be our biggest teachers
if we choose to reframe them that way.
There is always a lesson to be learned
that was meant to prepare you for the next stage.

APRIL 2023

MONDAY **10**

TUESDAY **11**

WEDNESDAY **12**

THURSDAY ◗ **13**

FRIDAY   14

SATURDAY   15

SUNDAY ORTHODOX EASTER   16

When you keep aiming, you'll always be proud
of your grit and determination.
Look back at how far you've already come,
and trust that your journey is only beginning.

APRIL 2023

MONDAY YOM HASHOAH (BEGINS AT SUNDOWN) **17**

TUESDAY **18**

WEDNESDAY **19**

THURSDAY ○ **20**

FRIDAY EID AL-FITR (BEGINS AT SUNDOWN)　　　　**21**

SATURDAY EARTH DAY　　　　**22**

SUNDAY　　　　**23**

To keep aiming is to pivot when something isn't working, to be adaptable, to try again, to keep aiming. It's the getting back up no matter how many times you've been knocked down—that's what's inspiring.

APRIL 2023

MONDAY   **24**

TUESDAY   ANZAC DAY (AUS / NZ)   **25**

WEDNESDAY   ADMINISTRATIVE PROFESSIONALS' DAY (US)   **26**

THURSDAY ◗   **27**

FRIDAY   **28**

SATURDAY   **29**

SUNDAY   **30**

**Life is full of peaks and valleys and wherever you are
on your journey is exactly where you need to be.
Take in the intrinsic magic around you and trust that
you have the power to create something truly special.**

Let others' limiting beliefs about you **fuel your fire** to burn through them.

MAY 2023

NOTES	SUNDAY	MONDAY	TUESDAY
		1 LABOUR DAY (AUS-QLD) EARLY MAY BANK HOLIDAY (UK) FIRST DAY OF ASIAN AMERICAN AND PACIFIC ISLANDER HERITAGE MONTH	**2**
	7	**8**	**9**
	14 MOTHER'S DAY (US / CAN)	**15**	**16**
	21	**22** VICTORIA DAY (CAN)	**23**
	28	**29** SPRING BANK HOLIDAY (UK) MEMORIAL DAY (US)	**30**

MAY 2023

WEDNESDAY	THURSDAY	FRIDAY	SATURDAY
3	4 ●	5	6
		CINCO DE MAYO	
10	11 ☽	12	13
17	18 ○	19	20
24	25	26 ☾	27
31			

"I find that in a world that sets a lot of limits, **socially and mentally,** it is important to question things, no matter your age or social condition. It is essential to your growth. Values and beliefs that you create through your own personal experience are what make you limitless."

NORA GHERBI

Founder of WHo CAREs!? Chronicles, Board member of Edeyo Foundation, Contributor to Conscious Magazine

MAY 2023

MONDAY LABOUR DAY (AUS–QLD) / EARLY MAY BANK HOLIDAY UK / FIRST DAY OF ASIAN AMERICAN AND PACIFIC ISLANDER HERITAGE MONTH

1

TUESDAY

2

WEDNESDAY

3

THURSDAY

4

FRIDAY CINCO DE MAYO

5

SATURDAY

6

SUNDAY

7

MAY 2023

MONDAY   8

TUESDAY   9

WEDNESDAY   10

THURSDAY   11

FRIDAY ☽ **12**

SATURDAY **13**

SUNDAY MOTHER'S DAY (US / CAN) **14**

Living without limits means breaking boundaries
and leaving your comfort zone behind.
Believe that you can achieve something greater
than what those around you are asking of you,
or even what you are asking of yourself.

MAY 2023

MONDAY   **15**

TUESDAY   **16**

WEDNESDAY   **17**

THURSDAY   **18**

FRIDAY ○   **19**

SATURDAY   **20**

SUNDAY   **21**

**When you have vision and purpose,
the sheer force and expansion of your dreams
will knock down any limiting beliefs
that stand in your way.**

MAY 2023

MONDAY VICTORIA DAY (CAN)   **22**

TUESDAY   **23**

WEDNESDAY   **24**

THURSDAY   **25**

FRIDAY   26

SATURDAY ◖   27

SUNDAY   28

When your vision and dream become bigger than your
fear, you become limitless. You realize that it's always
worth taking the risk. Even if it doesn't work out the way
you intended, the growth and knowledge gained will push
you in the right, and perhaps even better, direction.

Light the trail to your wildest dreams.

JUNE 2023

NOTES	SUNDAY	MONDAY	TUESDAY
	4	5	6
	11	12	13
○	18	19	20
	FATHER'S DAY (US / CAN / UK)	JUNETEENTH (US)	
	25 ◗	26	27

JUNE 2023

WEDNESDAY	THURSDAY	FRIDAY	SATURDAY
	1	2	3
	FIRST DAY OF PRIDE MONTH		
7	8	9	10
14	15	16	17
FLAG DAY (US)			
21	22	23	24
SUMMER SOLSTICE			
28	29	30	

"Being a trailblazer means paving the way for others. My advice is to always be yourself, and stand up for yourself and what you believe in. Surround yourself with positive and supportive people who encourage you to follow and achieve your dreams, no matter what."

AMANDA LEPORE

Transgender Model, Celebutante, Singer, and Performance Artist

JUNE 2023

MONDAY (MAY) SPRING BANK HOLIDAY (UK) / MEMORIAL DAY (US) — **29**

TUESDAY (MAY) — **30**

WEDNESDAY (MAY) — **31**

THURSDAY FIRST DAY OF PRIDE MONTH — **1**

FRIDAY — **2**

SATURDAY ● — **3**

SUNDAY — **4**

JUNE 2023

MONDAY 5

TUESDAY 6

WEDNESDAY 7

THURSDAY 8

FRIDAY   9

SATURDAY ☽   10

SUNDAY   11

Being a trailblazer is success beyond
material affirmation and financial gain.
It's about forging a new path into a better world and
pulling along as many people as you can in the process.

JUNE 2023

MONDAY 12

TUESDAY 13

WEDNESDAY FLAG DAY (US) 14

THURSDAY 15

FRIDAY   **16**

SATURDAY   **17**

SUNDAY   FATHER'S DAY (US / CAN / UK)   ○   **18**

You have the ability to blaze your own trail starting now.
Maybe it's standing up for yourself when someone
is putting you down, or maybe it's volunteering
to do charity work for a cause you are passionate about;
big changes start with small steps.

JUNE 2023

MONDAY JUNETEENTH HOLIDAY   **19**

TUESDAY   **20**

WEDNESDAY SUMMER SOLSTICE   **21**

THURSDAY   **22**

FRIDAY   23

SATURDAY   24

SUNDAY   25

When you are true to yourself, you inspire others
to move forward with a greater level of authenticity.
The world is a more interesting and beautiful place
when we embrace our individual purpose
and blaze a trail for a better future.

LIVE FEAR LESSLY

Don't let the **fear of trying** be greater than your fear of regret.

JULY 2023

NOTES	SUNDAY	MONDAY	TUESDAY
	2	3	4
			INDEPENDENCE DAY (US)
	9	10	11
	16	17	18
	23	24	25
	30	31	

JULY 2023

WEDNESDAY	THURSDAY	FRIDAY	SATURDAY
			1
			CANADA DAY (CAN)
5	6	7	8
12	13	14	15
19	20	21	22
26	27	28	29

"The best way to move through fear is not by planning every single thing that could go wrong, it's by just **engaging with the world.** Just doing it, even when you have no idea what you're doing."

JESSICA EKSTROM

Entrepreneur and Author, Founder of Headbands of Hope

JULY 2023

MONDAY (JUNE) ◖   **26**

TUESDAY (JUNE)   **27**

WEDNESDAY (JUNE)   **28**

THURSDAY (JUNE)   **29**

FRIDAY (JUNE)   **30**

SATURDAY   CANADA DAY (CAN)   **1**

SUNDAY   **2**

JULY 2023

MONDAY ● 3

TUESDAY INDEPENDENCE DAY (US) 4

WEDNESDAY 5

THURSDAY 6

FRIDAY 7

SATURDAY 8

SUNDAY ☽ 9

You'll be amazed at what starts to come to fruition
as you shut out the noise within
and become more fearless and focused.
Feel that fear, then do it anyway.

JULY 2023

MONDAY 10

TUESDAY 11

WEDNESDAY 12

THURSDAY 13

FRIDAY 14

SATURDAY 15

SUNDAY 16

Having a game plan and a fallback in place
to combat your fears will push you forward
despite the obstacles you'll face.

JULY 2023

MONDAY ○   **17**

TUESDAY   **18**

WEDNESDAY   **19**

THURSDAY   **20**

FRIDAY   **21**

SATURDAY   **22**

SUNDAY   **23**

We all have insights and experiences to share
that can help others, and when we focus
on the importance of the message we bring to the world
and our greater purpose, fear goes away.

JULY 2023

MONDAY   24

TUESDAY ◗   25

WEDNESDAY   26

THURSDAY   27

FRIDAY **28**

SATURDAY **29**

SUNDAY **30**

We all have a story to tell:
make yours one for the books.
Find your bliss and trust that the journey
will be wildly, joyously, *imperfectly* perfect.

RIDE THE WAVE

Though the waves of life, at times, make us feel like we'll drown, they also teach us how to swim, and remind us that we'll rise again.

AUGUST 2023

NOTES	SUNDAY	MONDAY	TUESDAY
			1
	6	7	8
	13	14	15
	20	21	22
	27	28	29

SUMMER BANK HOLIDAY
(UK-ENG / NIR / WAL)

AUGUST 2023

WEDNESDAY	THURSDAY	FRIDAY	SATURDAY
2	3	4	5
9	10	11	12
○ 16	17	18	19
23 ◗	24	25	26
● 30	31		

"Often our greatest difficulties
in life become our superpowers.
I used to think I couldn't be an actor
because I didn't want to be
the center of attention.
But being a quiet observer
has greatly served me
as a storyteller.
**Lean into what makes
you different.**
I've found that it always
ends up being what people
connect with most."

ESSA O'SHEA

Actor

AUGUST 2023

MONDAY (JULY)   **31**

TUESDAY ●   **1**

WEDNESDAY   **2**

THURSDAY   **3**

FRIDAY   **4**

SATURDAY   **5**

SUNDAY   **6**

AUGUST 2023

MONDAY 7

TUESDAY 8

WEDNESDAY 9

THURSDAY 10

FRIDAY   11

SATURDAY   12

SUNDAY   13

Life can and *will* throw you a curveball or plot twist
when you least expect it. Giving into flow,
learning that waves will crash and dissipate,
knock you down and lift you up, will help you
find solace in the fickle nature of life.

AUGUST 2023

MONDAY   14

TUESDAY   15

WEDNESDAY ○   16

THURSDAY   17

FRIDAY 18

SATURDAY 19

SUNDAY 20

Highs and lows are a natural part of life and success,
and the waves we experience
craft the rich, bold, monumental chapters in our story.

AUGUST 2023

MONDAY   21

TUESDAY   22

WEDNESDAY   23

THURSDAY   24

FRIDAY   25

SATURDAY   26

SUNDAY   27

Learning to ride the waves of life
is one of our ultimate purposes in this life;
it builds our character, it defines us, it makes us stronger.

The love we have for ourselves sets the bar for all the other love we experience. It starts with us.

SEPTEMBER 2023

NOTES	SUNDAY	MONDAY	TUESDAY
	3	**4**	**5**
	FATHER'S DAY (AUS / NZ)	LABOR DAY (US) LABOUR DAY (CAN)	
	10	**11**	**12**
	GRANDPARENTS' DAY (US)	PATRIOT DAY (US)	
	17	**18**	**19**
	24	**25**	**26**
	YOM KIPPUR (BEGINS AT SUNDOWN)		

SEPTEMBER 2023

WEDNESDAY	THURSDAY	FRIDAY	SATURDAY
		1	2
6	7	8	9
13	14	15	16
		ROSH HASHANAH (BEGINS AT SUNDOWN) FIRST DAY OF NATIONAL HISPANIC HERITAGE MONTH	
20	21	22	23
			FALL EQUINOX
27	28	29	30
		SUKKOT (BEGINS AT SUNDOWN)	

"**Being beautiful can mean so many things,** and I think that's something young girls need to know. You need to love yourself on every level. When you find confidence in your insecurities, you start to love all of yourself."

JESSICA IACULLO

Founder of Hungry Jess Big City

SEPTEMBER 2023

MONDAY (AUGUST) SUMMER BANK HOLIDAY (UK-ENG / NIR / WAL)   **28**

TUESDAY (AUGUST)   **29**

WEDNESDAY (AUGUST) ●   **30**

THURSDAY (AUGUST)   **31**

FRIDAY   **1**

SATURDAY   **2**

SUNDAY FATHER'S DAY (AUS / NZ)   **3**

SEPTEMBER 2023

MONDAY LABOR DAY (US) / LABOUR DAY (CAN)

4

TUESDAY

5

WEDNESDAY ☽

6

THURSDAY

7

FRIDAY   8

SATURDAY   9

SUNDAY GRANDPARENTS' DAY (US)   10

> You are worthy of your own love. Love yourself
> even on your worst days because you—yes, *you*—
> are enough no matter what. When you own who you are,
> that's when the magic happens.

SEPTEMBER 2023

MONDAY PATRIOT DAY (US) **11**

TUESDAY **12**

WEDNESDAY **13**

THURSDAY ○ **14**

FRIDAY ROSH HASHANAH (BEGINS AT SUNDOWN) / FIRST DAY OF NATIONAL HISPANIC HERITAGE MONTH   **15**

SATURDAY   **16**

SUNDAY   **17**

Do things that expand your mind, body, and soul.
Set aside non-negotiable "me" time each week
to reset yourself, whether it's a weekly bubble bath
with a glass of wine, journaling, trying a new recipe,
or getting out in nature.

SEPTEMBER 2023

MONDAY 18

TUESDAY 19

WEDNESDAY 20

THURSDAY 21

FRIDAY ◑   **22**

SATURDAY FALL EQUINOX   **23**

SUNDAY YOM KIPPUR (BEGINS AT SUNDOWN)   **24**

To love ourselves is to not settle for less than we deserve;
it's prioritizing healthy habits and self-care, striving to
show up as the best possible version of ourselves,
and knowing we must fill our own cup
before we can fill others'.

YOU'VE GOT THIS

Realize
your own potential
and become
unstoppable.

OCTOBER 2023

NOTES	SUNDAY	MONDAY	TUESDAY
		1	2
		LABOUR DAY (AUS-ACT / NSW / SA)	3
	8	9	10
		INDIGENOUS PEOPLES' DAY (US) COLUMBUS DAY (US) THANKSGIVING DAY (CAN)	
	15	16	17
	22	23	24
		LABOUR DAY (NZ)	
	29	30	31
			HALLOWEEN

OCTOBER 2023

WEDNESDAY	THURSDAY	FRIDAY	SATURDAY
4	5	6	7
			SIMCHAT TORAH (BEGINS AT SUNDOWN)
11	12	13	14
18	19	20	21
25	26	27	28

"Literally,
tell yourself out loud
that you're up to your challenges.
When you say something out loud,
your subconscious believes
that it's true."

KRISTINA LOPEZ ADDUCI

Founder and CEO of House of Puff and Art Zealous

OCTOBER 2023

MONDAY (SEPTEMBER)   **25**

TUESDAY (SEPTEMBER)   **26**

WEDNESDAY (SEPTEMBER)   **27**

THURSDAY (SEPTEMBER)   **28**

FRIDAY (SEPTEMBER)   SUKKOT (BEGINS AT SUNDOWN) ●   **29**

SATURDAY (SEPTEMBER)   **30**

SUNDAY   **1**

OCTOBER 2023

MONDAY LABOUR DAY (AUS-ACT / NSW / SA)   2

TUESDAY   3

WEDNESDAY   4

THURSDAY   5

FRIDAY ☽ 6

SATURDAY SIMCHAT TORAH (BEGINS AT SUNDOWN) 7

SUNDAY 8

Trust that you can do the hard things. You are capable of overcoming whatever disappointments, setbacks, or heartbreaks come up. You have the power to accomplish whatever you set your mind to, and you deserve to live out your biggest dreams.

OCTOBER 2023

MONDAY INDIGENOUS PEOPLES' DAY (US) / COLUMBUS DAY (US) / THANKSGIVING DAY (CAN) **9**

TUESDAY **10**

WEDNESDAY **11**

THURSDAY **12**

FRIDAY   13

SATURDAY ○   14

SUNDAY   15

Change negative thoughts into positive affirmations.
The next time you catch yourself falling into the trap
of questioning your abilities, close your eyes and say,
"I can do this." Breathe it into existence.

OCTOBER 2023

MONDAY 16

TUESDAY 17

WEDNESDAY 18

THURSDAY 19

FRIDAY 20

SATURDAY 21

SUNDAY 22

Success can mean so many things and it's your purpose in life to define what it means to you. Believe that you have the power to make it happen and get out of your own way.

OCTOBER 2023

MONDAY LABOUR DAY (NZ) — 23

TUESDAY — 24

WEDNESDAY — 25

THURSDAY — 26

FRIDAY   27

SATURDAY ●   28

SUNDAY   29

When we adopt an attitude of collaboration
over competition, when we realize others' success
doesn't dampen our own, when we approach others
with love and genuine connection—
that's when we all truly thrive.

Have the courage to hustle for your dreams and hustle harder for what **ignites your soul.**

NOVEMBER 2023

NOTES	SUNDAY	MONDAY	TUESDAY
	☽ 5	6	7
	DAYLIGHT SAVING TIME ENDS (US / CAN)		ELECTION DAY (US)
	12 ○	13	14
	19 ☾	20	21
	26 ●	27	28

NOVEMBER 2023

WEDNESDAY	THURSDAY	FRIDAY	SATURDAY
1 ALL SAINTS' DAY	2	3	4
8	9	10	11 VETERANS DAY (US)
15	16	17	18
22	23 THANKSGIVING DAY (US)	24 NATIVE AMERICAN HERITAGE DAY (US)	25
29	30		

"Go day by day
and do everything
in your power to
work toward your goals.
I try to stay conscious
of not letting overthinking
fully paralyze me into
never doing anything at all."

DANI EGNA

Founder and CEO of Inked by Dani

NOVEMBER 2023

MONDAY (OCTOBER) 30

TUESDAY (OCTOBER) HALLOWEEN 31

WEDNESDAY ALL SAINTS' DAY 1

THURSDAY 2

FRIDAY 3

SATURDAY 4

SUNDAY DAYLIGHT SAVING TIME ENDS (US / CAN) 5

NOVEMBER 2023

MONDAY 6

TUESDAY ELECTION DAY (US) 7

WEDNESDAY 8

THURSDAY 9

FRIDAY 10

SATURDAY VETERANS DAY (US) 11

SUNDAY 12

Hustling isn't just an action, it's a state of mind.
It's that scrappy, can-do, whatever-it-takes attitude
that only our deepest passions can engender.

NOVEMBER 2023

MONDAY ○   **13**

TUESDAY   **14**

WEDNESDAY   **15**

THURSDAY   **16**

FRIDAY   17

SATURDAY   18

SUNDAY   19

Build equity in yourself.
You will never regret working hard at something
that makes you proud and builds your future.

NOVEMBER 2023

MONDAY ◐ **20**

TUESDAY **21**

WEDNESDAY **22**

THURSDAY THANKSGIVING DAY (US) **23**

FRIDAY NATIVE AMERICAN HERITAGE DAY (US)   **24**

SATURDAY   **25**

SUNDAY   **26**

To truly hustle is to be willing to work your butt off,
take risks that terrify you, and know when
to set boundaries so you don't burn out.

WILD
FLOWER

Be ever growing, evolving, transforming, and becoming.

DECEMBER 2023

NOTES	SUNDAY	MONDAY	TUESDAY
	3	**4** ☽	**5**
	INTERNATIONAL DAY OF PERSONS WITH DISABILITIES		
	10	**11** ○	**12**
	HUMAN RIGHTS DAY		
	17	**18** ☾	**19**
	24	**25** ●	**26**
	CHRISTMAS EVE		BOXING DAY (UK / CAN / AUS / NZ)
	31		
	NEW YEAR'S EVE	CHRISTMAS DAY	KWANZAA

DECEMBER 2023

WEDNESDAY	THURSDAY	FRIDAY	SATURDAY
		1 WORLD AIDS DAY	**2**
6	**7** HANUKKAH (BEGINS AT SUNDOWN)	**8**	**9**
13	**14**	**15**	**16**
20	**21** WINTER SOLSTICE	**22**	**23**
27	**28**	**29**	**30**

"I wouldn't tell my younger self anything—all of my life experiences have value. As challenging or as joyful as they are, they **build on one another.** A preview or sneak peek on how to live or what to do could cheat you out of experiences that are critical."

LO BOSWORTH

Founder and CEO of Love Wellness

DECEMBER 2023

MONDAY (NOVEMBER) ●   **27**

TUESDAY (NOVEMBER)   **28**

WEDNESDAY (NOVEMBER)   **29**

THURSDAY (NOVEMBER)   **30**

FRIDAY   WORLD AIDS DAY   **1**

SATURDAY   **2**

SUNDAY   INTERNATIONAL DAY OF PERSONS WITH DISABILITIES   **3**

DECEMBER 2023

MONDAY 4

TUESDAY ☽ 5

WEDNESDAY 6

THURSDAY HANUKKAH (BEGINS AT SUNDOWN) 7

FRIDAY   8

SATURDAY   9

SUNDAY   HUMAN RIGHTS DAY   10

Every day we're growing, evolving, and changing.
Just as wildflowers bloom through different seasons,
we must welcome transition and trust
that we too will establish our roots.

DECEMBER 2023

MONDAY   **11**

TUESDAY ○   **12**

WEDNESDAY   **13**

THURSDAY   **14**

FRIDAY 15

SATURDAY 16

SUNDAY 17

When you give yourself permission to be wild and grow freely, you don't let labels or expectations define you or keep you small. You grow into the woman of your own dreams, blooming far beyond what you had imagined.

DECEMBER 2023

MONDAY   **18**

TUESDAY ◑   **19**

WEDNESDAY   **20**

THURSDAY WINTER SOLSTICE   **21**

FRIDAY 22

SATURDAY 23

SUNDAY CHRISTMAS EVE 24

You have room to grow no matter where you are in life. If you don't like your situation or you want more for yourself, you can do it. We are all wildflowers blooming into our next opportunity, our next transition.

DECEMBER 2023

MONDAY CHRISTMAS DAY   **25**

TUESDAY BOXING DAY (UK / CAN / AUS / NZ) / KWANZAA ● **26**

WEDNESDAY   **27**

THURSDAY   **28**

FRIDAY **29**

SATURDAY **30**

SUNDAY NEW YEAR'S EVE **31**

Give yourself love, time, and attention.
A wildflower doesn't grow overnight;
it slowly expands into the beauty that it is.
It blooms in light, and so do you.

NOTES

NOTES

NOTES

NOTES

NOTES

NOTES

Inspiring | Educating | Creating | Entertaining

Brimming with creative inspiration, how-to projects, and useful information to enrich your everyday life, quarto.com is a favorite destination for those pursuing their interests and passions.

First published in 2022 by Rock Point, an imprint of The Quarto Group,
142 West 36th Street, 4th Floor, New York, NY 10018, USA
T (212) 779-4972 F (212) 779-6058 www.Quarto.com

Contains content previously published in 2021 as *Follow Your Bliss* by Rock Point,
an imprint of The Quarto Group, 142 West 36th Street, 4th Floor, New York, NY 10018,

Rock Point titles are also available at discount for retail, wholesale, promotional, and bulk purchase. For details, contact the Special Sales Manager by email at specialsales@quarto.com or by mail at The Quarto Group, Attn: Special Sales Manager, 100 Cummings Center Suite 265D, Beverly, MA 01915 USA.

10 9 8 7 6 5 4 3 2 1

ISBN: 978-1-63106-903-1

Publisher: Rage Kindelsperger
Creative Director: Laura Drew
Managing Editor: Cara Donaldson
Project Editor: Sara Bonacum
Cover and Interior Design: Evelin Kasikov
Layout Design: Danielle Smith-Boldt

This planner provides general information on various widely known and widely accepted images that tend to evoke feelings of strength and confidence. However, it should not be relied upon as recommending or promoting any specific diagnosis or method of treatment for a particular condition, and it is not intended as a substitute for medical advice or for direct diagnosis and treatment of a medical condition by a qualified physician. Readers who have questions about a particular condition, possible treatments for that condition, or possible reactions from the condition or its treatment should consult a physician or other qualified healthcare professional.

All moon phases shown are for the Eastern Time Zone.

Printed in China